Meet Mouse and Moose

By Michael Harry

Illustrated by Mary Collier

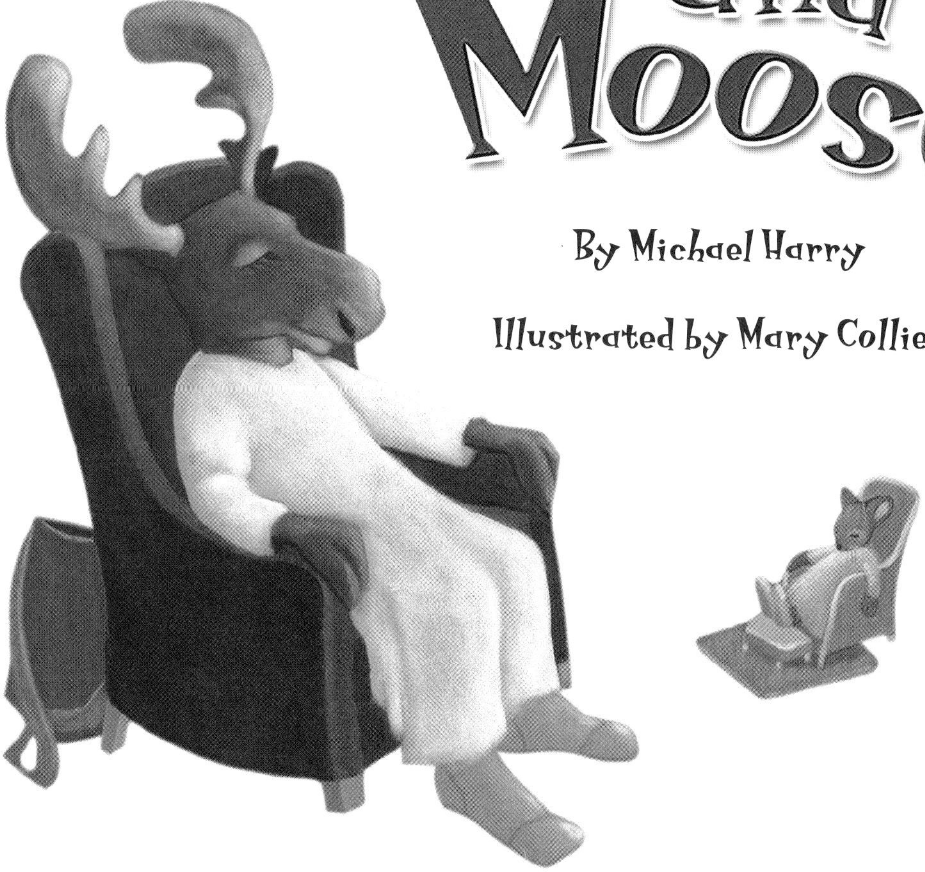

Target Skill Consonant *Mm*/m/

Scott Foresman
is an imprint of
PEARSON

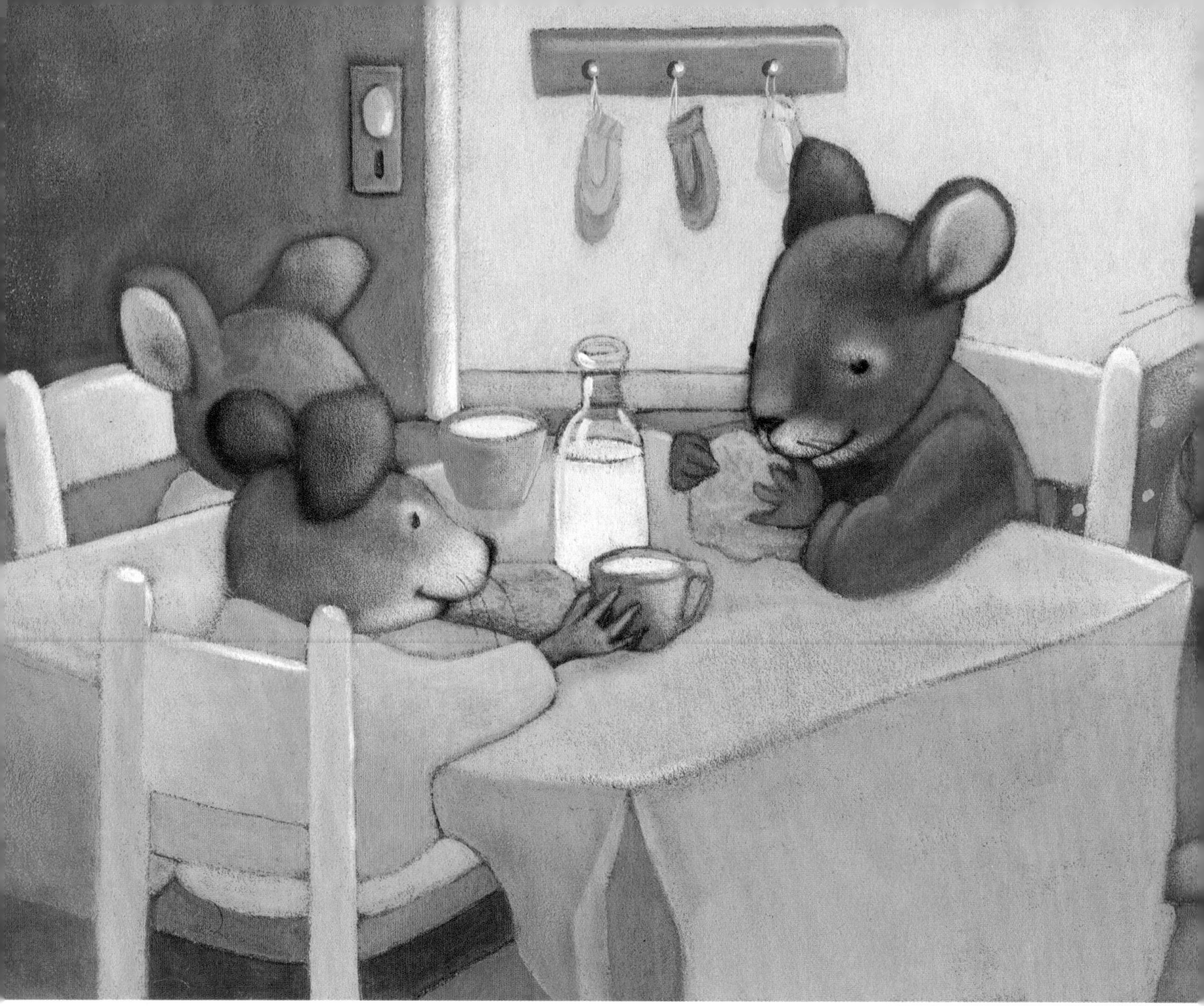

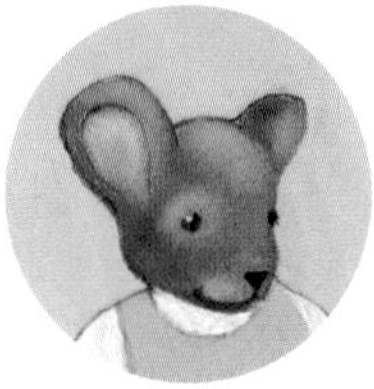

mouse

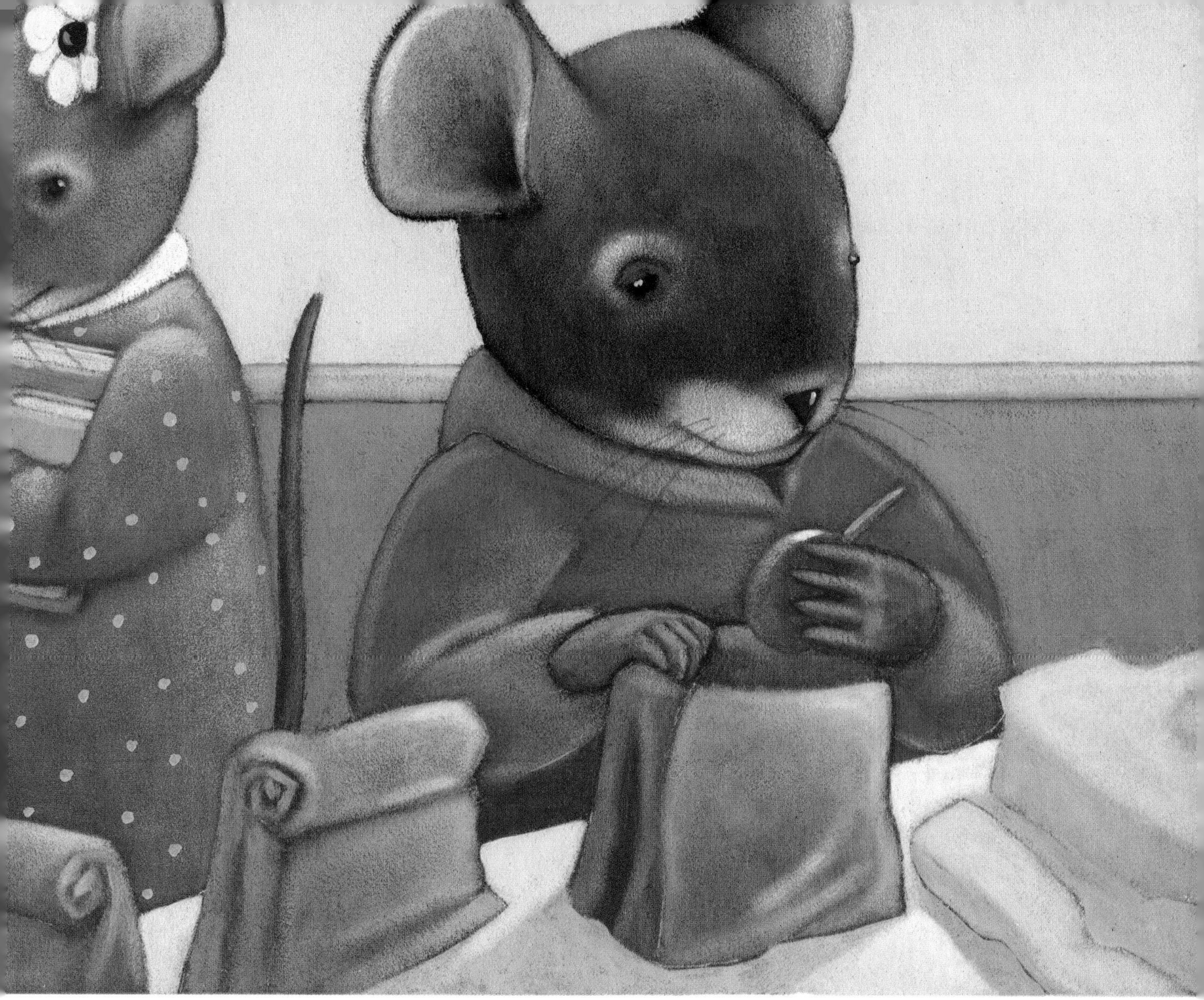

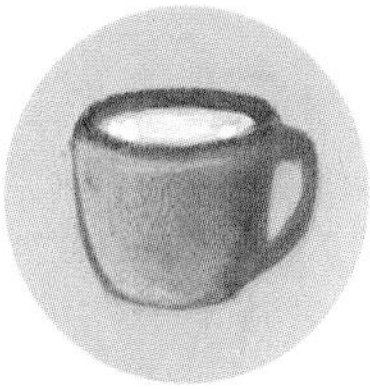

mug

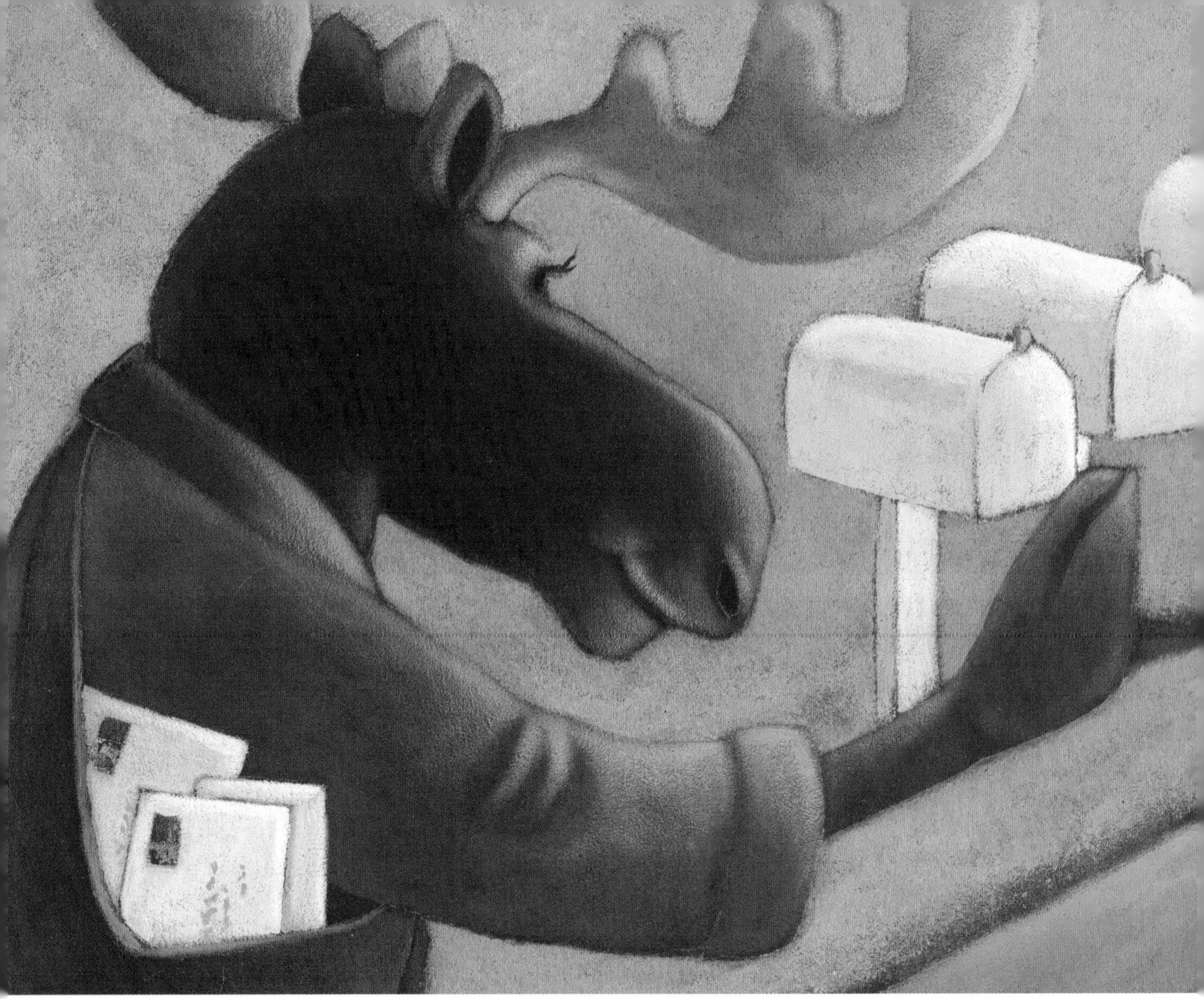

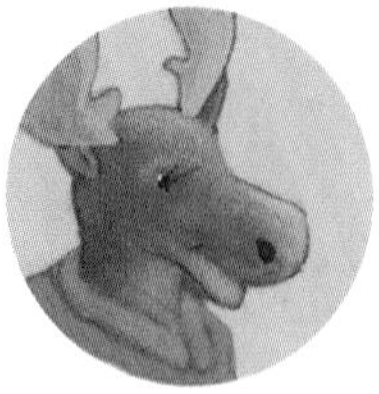

moose

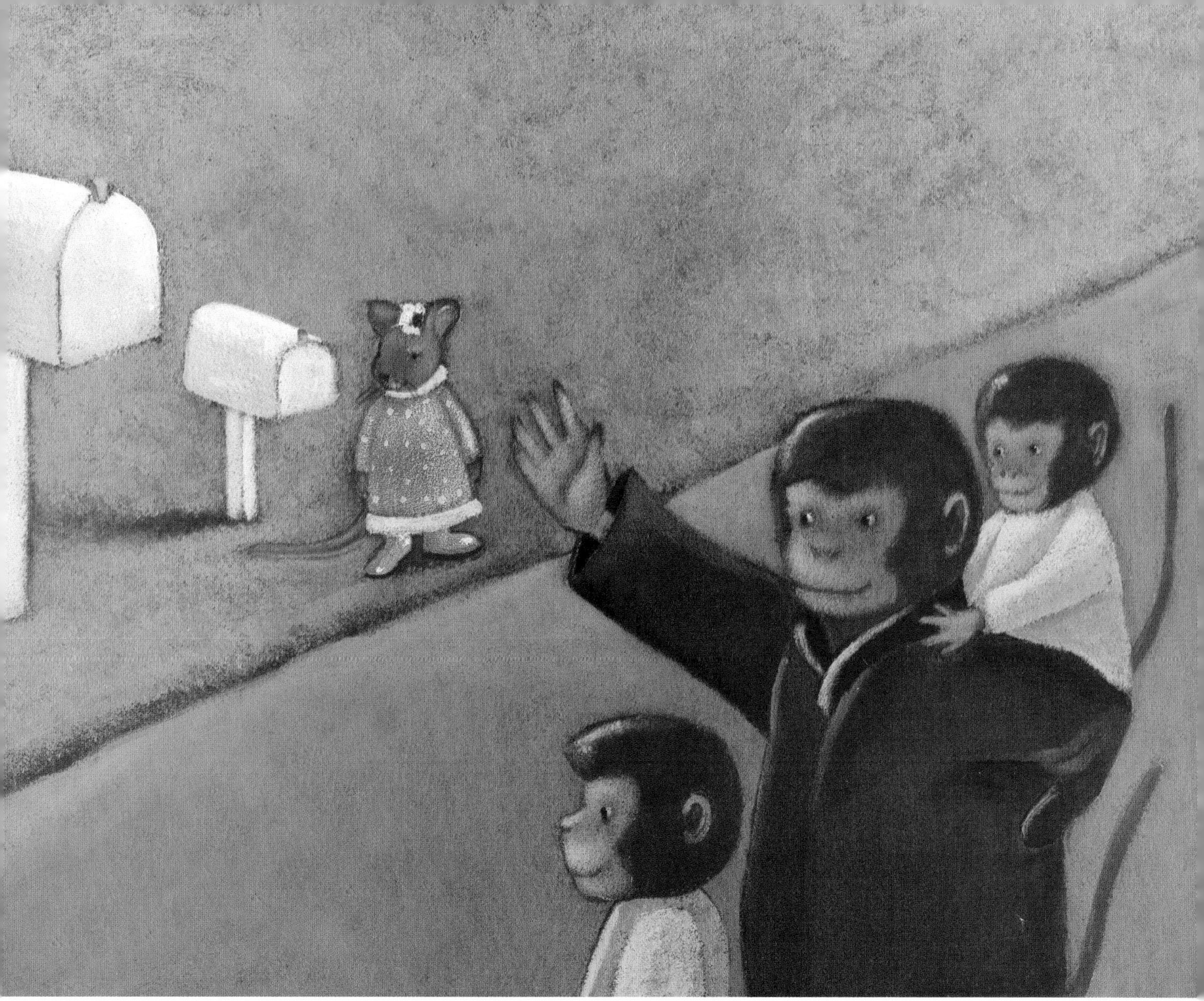

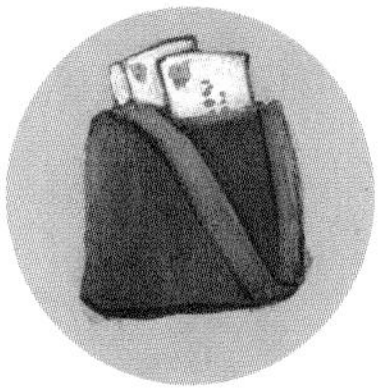

mail

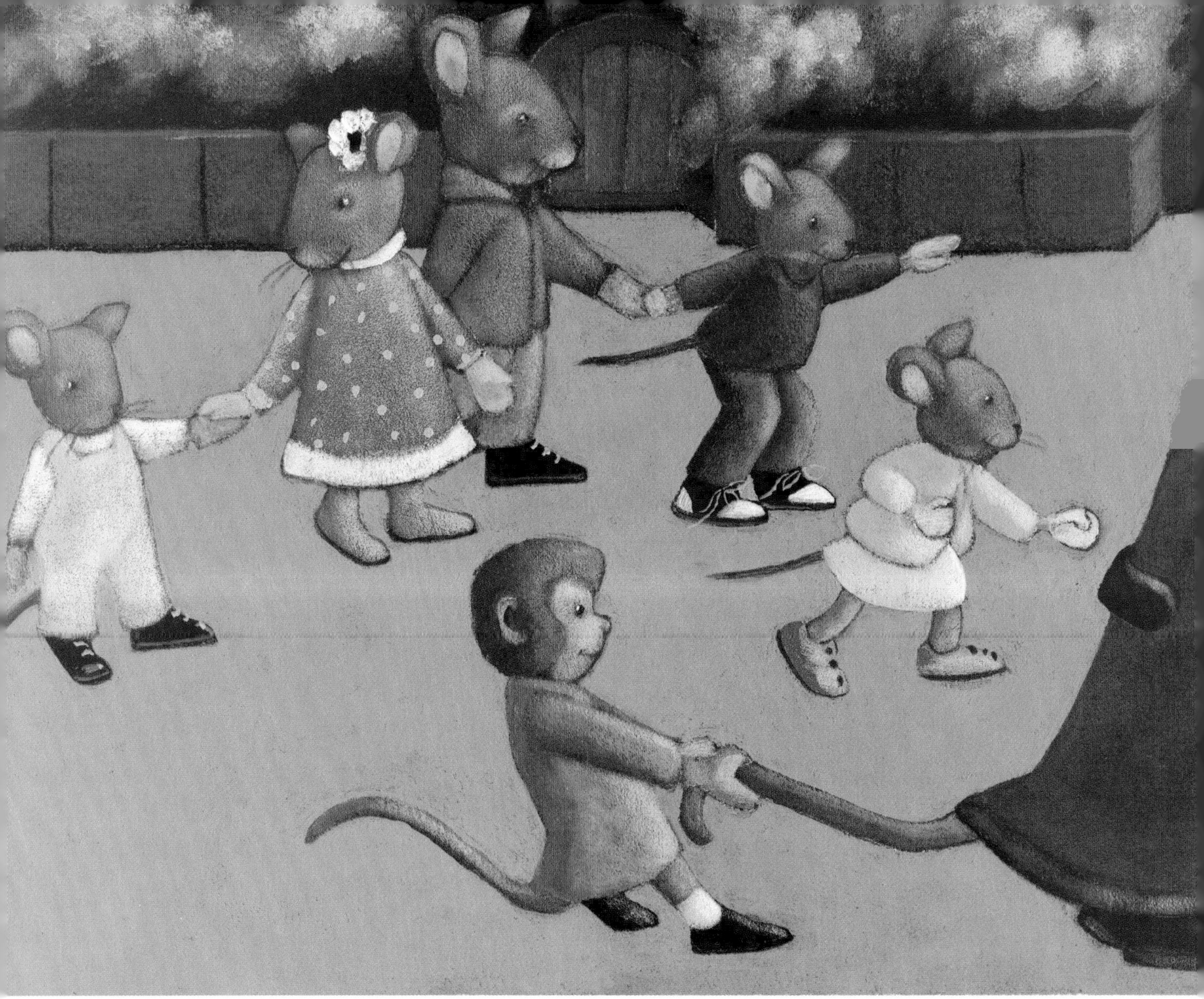

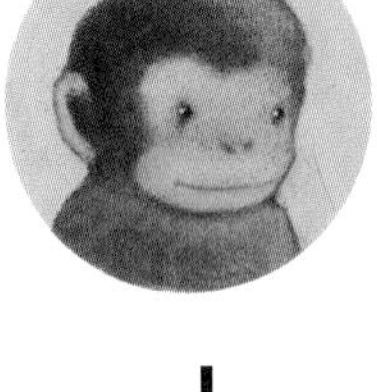

monkey

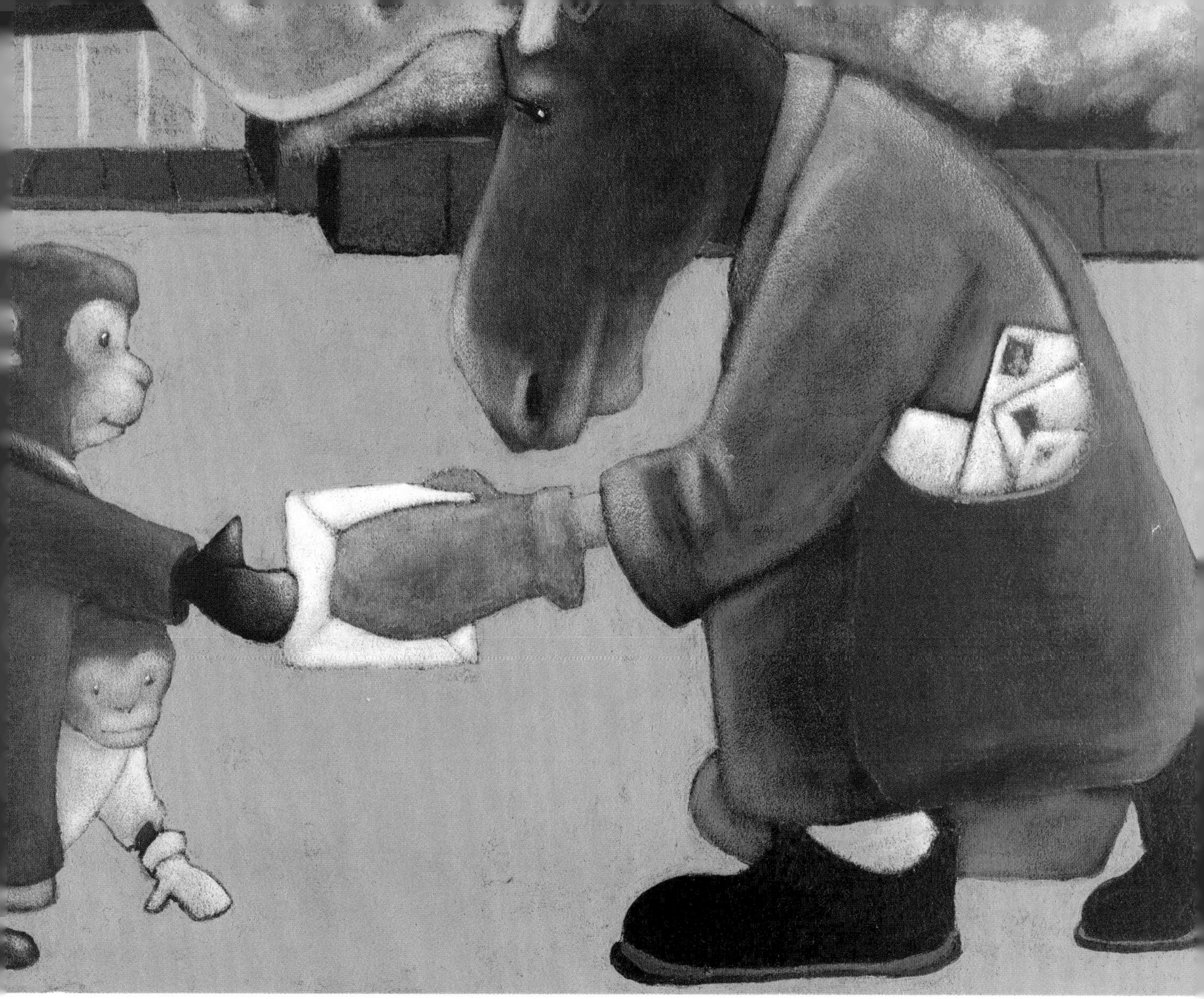

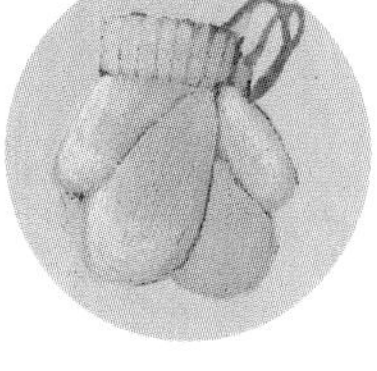

mittens

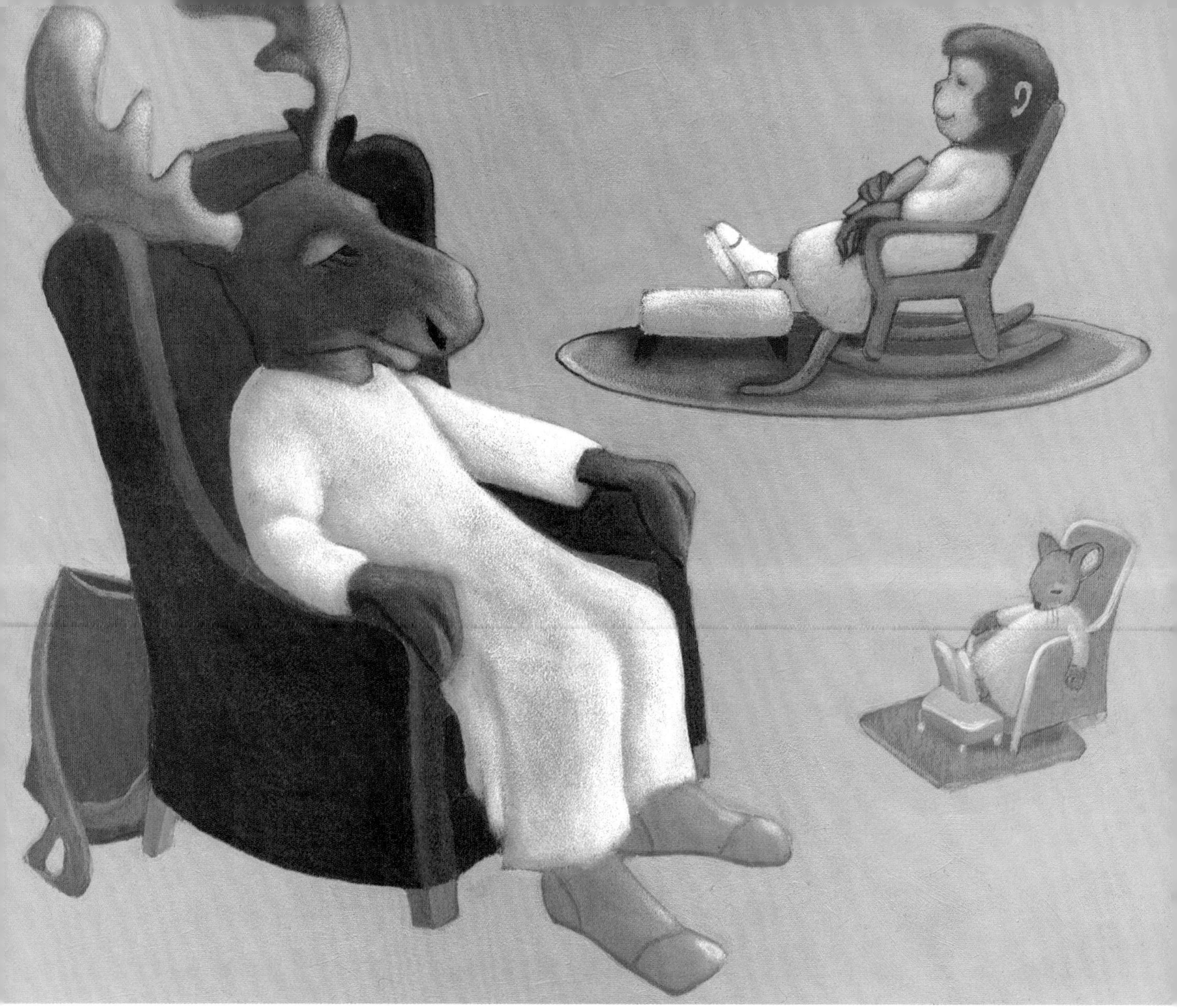

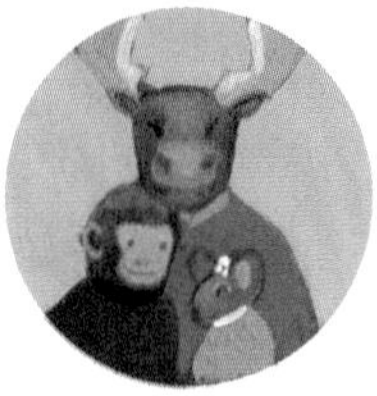

mom